THE GRACE OF GOD

THE GRACE OF GOD

Tony Evans

MOODY PUBLISHERS
CHICAGO

Developmental Editor: Phil Rawley
Copy Editor: Cheryl Dunlop
Interior Design: Ragont Design
Cover Design: Smartt Guys design
Cover Image: Jeremy Walker/The Image Bank

Library of Congress Cataloging-in-Publication Data

Evans, Anthony T.
The grace of God / Tony Evans.
p. cm.
ISBN 978-0-8024-4380-9
1. Grace (Theology) I. Title.

BT761.3.E87 2004
234--dc22

2004001880

We hope you enjoy this book from Moody Publishers. Our goal is to provide high-quality, thought-provoking books and products that connect truth to your real needs and challenges. For more information on other books and products written and produced from a biblical perspective, go to www.moodypublishers.com or write to:

Moody Publishers
820 N. LaSalle Boulevard
Chicago, IL 60610

3 5 7 9 10 8 6 4

Printed in the United States of America

CONTENTS

1

The Concept of Grace

A man who had been born and raised in a country ruled by a strict military dictatorship immigrated to the United States and became a citizen of this country.

The man decided to celebrate his new citizenship by doing some sightseeing around the city where he was living. He was enjoying himself so much that he didn't notice that sundown was approaching. But as soon as the sunlight faded and darkness began to descend, the new American panicked.

He ran up to a car and begged the driver to take him home as quickly as possible. The driver was taken aback and tried to calm the man down. When asked why he had to get home so quickly, the man cried out, "Because I don't want to violate curfew and be arrested."

The problem was that in the man's previous country, the military had imposed a strict curfew. Everyone had to be off the streets by sundown or risk arrest.

The man in the car smiled when he realized the problem. He calmly explained that since the United States has no curfew, the man wasn't in any trouble. The new citizen simply had not yet learned to cast off the bondage of the old country. He was free, but he wasn't living like it.

A lot of Christians, citizens of heaven who have been set free by the grace of God in Christ, have not learned how to cast off the bondage of their birth in Adam. They sing and talk about freedom, but they are living under an oppressive system of religious rules that sends them running home at sundown, so to speak.

WHEN YOU GOT SAVED, YOU WERE BROUGHT INTO A NEW REGIME.

This oppressive religious system is called legalism, and it's absolutely contrary to our freedom in Christ. But many Christians are being held hostage to the old regime.

If there is one overarching truth I want to get across to you in this booklet, it is this: When you got saved, you were brought into a new regime. *You have been liberated by God's magnificent grace, and the old rules no longer apply.*

Now I realize that applying the truth we know can be another story. So we need to understand what legalism is, and how it shackles us, before we can understand how to break its chains and fully appreciate the freedom we possess in Christ.

The Bible goes to great lengths to combat legalism and establish us in grace. So let's find out how to shed the shackles and be truly free.

THE BONDAGE OF LEGALISM

The apostle Paul gives us a definition of legalism in Galatians 3:3, stated in the form of a question. "Having begun by the Spirit, are you now being perfected by the flesh?"

Legalism is trying to please God "by the flesh," by attempting to keep a list of laws and rules that we think will earn us God's favor and keep us in good standing with Him. It is identity based on performance rather than relationship. It makes rule-keeping the basis of spiritual victory.

The problem with this should be obvious. We can't earn our salvation. We didn't begin with Christ by doing works of the flesh but by the grace of God administered by the Holy Spirit.

This is such a serious matter that Paul used the strongest language possible in addressing the Galatians, who had fallen victim to legalism. He began his letter by saying, "I am amazed that you are so quickly deserting Him who called you by the grace of Christ, for a different gospel" (Galatians 1:6). Even though Paul called legalism a "gospel," he was using the word to shock his readers. He quickly added that it was not really another gospel but a distortion of the true message (v. 7).

You see, wherever Paul went he was followed by Jewish teachers called Judaizers, who sought to subject Gentile Christians to the bondage of the Law of Moses (Galatians 2:4; see also 5:10). This is why Paul used such strong language. "You foolish Galatians, who has bewitched you, before whose eyes Jesus Christ was publicly portrayed as crucified?" (3:1). The answer was the Judaizers.

A FEW GOOD QUESTIONS

Then Paul asked another series of questions in Galatians 3:2–5, all of which contrast grace with works. The correct answer in each case is that the Christian life, symbolized by the giving of the Holy Spirit, is of grace and not of works.

> GRACE-BASED CHRISTIANS OBEY BECAUSE IT'S THEIR DELIGHT.

Allow me to ask you a few questions. Were you saved by keeping the Ten Commandments? Are you going to heaven because you're better than your neighbor? Are you hoping to please God by trying your very hardest to be good?

I hope your answer to each of these is no, because no one will ever be saved or please God by these means.

When you try to mix human effort with God's grace, you're trying to mix oil and water.

Now, don't misunderstand me. Legalism is not merely the *presence* of the Law. God's Law is "holy and righteous and good" (Romans 7:12). The problem is that the Law provides no power to obey it.

Legalism is not the presence of rules but the wrong *attitude* toward the rules. Legalism assigns to the rules a power to produce obedience that God never gave them. Victory and true liberty cannot be found in human effort.

A GUILT-DRIVEN SYSTEM

You see, legalism is a guilt-motivated system. We either allow others to put us in bondage to their list of rules, or we shackle ourselves to our own list.

Here's how it works. A Christian who tends toward legalism goes to church one Sunday and hears the preacher say, "You need to read your Bible and pray." This Christian feels guilty because he hasn't been reading his Bible and praying. So he sets his alarm back an hour that night. But when the alarm goes off the next morning, this guy doesn't really want to get up. He's kind of grumpy, but he dutifully staggers out of bed to read his Bible and pray because he feels that he has to.

Is there anything wrong with a preacher telling his people they ought to read their Bibles and pray? No, and I'll be the first one to say it. And it's not necessarily bad that this Christian feels guilty for neglecting his spiritual life. That could be the conviction of the Holy Spirit. The problem comes in the way he deals with his need.

Grace-based Christians obey because it's their delight. Law-based Christians obey because it's their duty. Grace-based Christians obey and love it. Law-based Christians obey and resent it. To grace-based Christians, the spiritual life is the lifting of a burden (see Matthew 11:30). But to legalistic Christians, living for God feels like carrying a heavy load.

Suppose both partners in a marriage carried around checklists of each other's duties and checked each duty off as it was done. If the whole marriage worked on that basis, I'd soon be seeing that couple in my office for counseling.

Husbands and wives who love each other help each other, but the doing has to grow out of the loving. God wants nothing less from us. If your Christian life is just a list, you're missing it—not necessarily because the things on your list are bad. It's just that living by a list is a faulty approach to victory in the Christian life.

THE CONFUSION BEHIND LEGALISM

Now that we know something about the nature of legalism, we need to ask an important question. If spiritual legalism is so confining and guilt-producing, why are so many Christians falling into this trap?

In many cases, the answer is that believers are confused about this fundamental truth: "Sin shall not be master over you, for you are not under law but under grace" (Romans 6:14).

A lot of Christians would say, "Come on, Tony, I know that. That's one of the most basic principles of the Christian life. I'm not confused about that."

But I have to wonder how many believers really understand grace. If they did, they would realize they are free to follow Christ. But freedom scares some folk, like the freed slaves who wanted to stay with their slave masters because slavery was all they had ever known.

God wants us to understand that we are completely *free* from the Law. Not free to live any way we want, but free from trying to save ourselves by measuring up to God's perfect standard.

In Romans 7:1–4, Paul used the death of a spouse to illustrate our freedom from the Law. A woman whose husband has died is free to remarry. The Law was our old "husband," but that relationship is dead, and we are in a new union with Christ. "Therefore, my brethren, you also were made to die to the Law through the body of Christ, so that you might be joined to another, to Him who was raised from the dead" (v. 4). A Christian who is trying to please God by legalism while joined to Christ in grace is living an absurdity.

It's like the woman who went on a trip to Europe after her husband died and she had gone through a period of grieving. On the trip she met a wonderful man. They fell in love, got married, and came back to the United States to live in her house.

But when the happy newlyweds arrived home, the man's jaw dropped. Propped up on the living room sofa was the corpse of the woman's first husband. She quickly explained, "I love you, but you must understand; I lived with this man for so long that I can't really function without him. I need to keep him nearby."

The woman's new husband let her know in no uncertain terms that he wasn't about to live with a dead man in the house. She would have to choose between her deceased husband and her new love.

I told you this was an absurdity! But this is what we do spiritually when we try to live by the Law after Christ has forgiven and received us by grace. Let's bury that corpse and move on, because mixing law and grace will never work.

If many believers are confused about the true relationship between law and grace, some are also confused about the nature and the role of God's Law.

The first thing we need to restate and reinforce is that the problem is not in the Law itself. The Law of God is good—but if it can't save us, what is its purpose? Paul gave its purpose in Galatians 3:24. "The Law has become our tutor to lead us to Christ, so that we may be justified by faith."

The apostle also explained with a personal example in Romans 7:7–11. Paul's problem was coveting. He didn't feel the sinfulness of coveting until the Law told him, "You shall not covet." But he also discovered that law gave him no power to obey God. He found himself coveting worse than ever.

In other words, the Law doesn't exist to make us better but to show us how helpless we are so that we will run to Christ. The Law is the speed-limit sign on the highway. It can't force you to slow down, but it gives the police officer the authority to write you a ticket when you fail to meet the standard.

The Law also arouses sin (see Romans 7:8). By arousing the sinful nature we had before we came to Christ, the Law showed us how much we needed Christ. But the Law serves the same function for us now that we know Christ. Our old nature may be dead in Christ, but our new nature is still encased in a sin-ravaged body called the flesh. And our flesh still wants to rebel against God.

The Law is the mirror that shows us how bad we look without Christ. But a mirror doesn't comb our hair or brush our teeth. The Law reveals God's good and perfect standard and shows us how messed up we are, but the Law can't fix what it reveals.

THE CONSEQUENCES OF LEGALISM

When you came to Jesus Christ, you died to the Law, so that it no longer has any authority over you. But the legalist who casts aside that freedom and puts himself back under the Law suffers the consequences. Paul explained in Galatians 5:

> It was for freedom that Christ set us free; therefore keep standing firm and do not be subject again to a yoke of slavery. Behold I, Paul, say to you that if you receive circumcision, Christ will be of no benefit to you. And I testify again to every man who receives circumcision, that he is under obligation to keep the whole Law. You have been severed from Christ, you who are seeking to be justified by law; you have fallen from grace. (vv. 1–4)

Legalism puts people under an impossible load. Who could possibly keep the whole Law? One consequence of legalism is the joyless bondage of trying harder, yet continually falling short.

Another consequence is even more serious. What does it mean to be "severed from Christ" and "fallen from grace"? These are two ways of saying the same thing. Legalism cuts us off from the flow of God's grace.

> IT IS LOVE THAT SUSTAINS A GODLY LIFE.

It's no coincidence that cult leaders control their people by putting them in bondage to their list of dos and don'ts. Pretty soon the followers are so dependent on the leader that they're incapable of relating to God or anyone else on their own.

Legalists have the same basic problem. That is, they never know when they've done enough to earn God's favor. Legalism takes you backward in your relationship with God. It is not a way to please God but a problem to be corrected.

THE CORRECTION FOR LEGALISM

Simply stated, the way to correct legalism is to maintain a relationship with God based on grace. Now, let me emphasize that such a relationship does not mean the absence of rules. It means that the rules grow out of the relationship, rather than being the basis of the relationship. It is love that sustains a godly life (see John 14:15; 1 John 5:3).

When God saved you, He wrote His Law in your heart and mind (Hebrews 10:16). He wants to relate to you from the inside. What was previously merely an external code is now a matter of the heart, and it comes with the desire to obey and please God.

Paul explained in 2 Corinthians 3:7–13 that when Moses came down from Mount Sinai with the old covenant, or the Law, his face glowed with God's glory. But the glory faded, so Moses had to hide his face behind a veil.

But the new covenant of God's grace isn't like that. The Bible says, "Now the Lord is the Spirit, and where the Spirit of the Lord is, there is liberty. But we all, with unveiled face, beholding as in a mirror the glory of the Lord, are being transformed into the same image from glory to glory, just as from the Lord, the Spirit" (2 Corinthians 3:17–18).

In the new covenant, Christ comes to live within us and brings His unfading glory. If we will keep our eyes on Christ, His glory will rub off on us and produce glory within us.

2

SAVED BY GRACE

Anyone who has truly tasted of God's grace will not want to go back to the Law. That's why the great Christian apologist and author C. S. Lewis said what he did when he walked into a room one day where a group of men were debating what makes Christianity unique among all the world's religions.

When the question was posed to him, Lewis answered right away. "That's easy. It's grace." Then he went on to explain that no other religion teaches the concept of a God who takes the initiative to respond with undeserved favor to sinners.

The good news of Christianity is what God has done to bridge the gap of sin and make it possible for sinful human beings to have forgiveness and fellowship with

Him. Now that we have explored the concept of grace, I want to consider what it means to be saved by grace.

A Definition of Grace

Theologians have developed a classic definition of grace as God's unmerited, or undeserved, favor toward sinners. I define grace as the inexhaustible supply of God's goodness whereby He does for us what we could never do for ourselves. It is His gift to us.

Since all of God's dealings with us are anchored in His grace, to miss grace is to miss God's activity in history. We are saved by grace, and the only way we grow as Christians is by grace.

Any serious study of grace will soon take us to Paul's great letter to the Ephesians. Paul used the word *grace* twelve times in this letter, beginning with his trademark salutation, "Grace to you" (1:2).

Then the apostle said, "[God] predestined us to adoption as sons through Jesus Christ to Himself, according to the kind intention of His will, to the praise of the glory of His grace, which He freely bestowed on us in the Beloved" (1:5–6). The only motivation for this outpouring of grace is God's kindness, which is why we will be praising God throughout eternity.

Sometimes we need to look back and remember where we once were before we can appreciate where we are today. One of the great problems in our culture is that folk who have "arrived" forget where they started.

When this happens people begin thinking that they deserve all the stuff they have, and they stop thanking and start demanding.

SETTING GRACE AGAINST A DARK BACKGROUND

Maybe we should have a "Remembrance Day" every so often in church, during which we go back to where we were before Christ and remember how hard and hopeless it was without Him, so we can learn to value grace more. Your appreciation of grace will soar, and your spiritual growth will be helped, when you see where God brought you from. Paul wrote:

> You were dead in your trespasses and sins, in which you formerly walked according to the course of this world, according to the prince of the power of the air, of the spirit that is now working in the sons of disobedience. Among them we too all formerly lived in the lusts of our flesh, indulging the desires of the flesh and of the mind, and were by nature the children of wrath, even as the rest. (Ephesians 2:1–3)

Several years ago, when my wife, Lois, and I celebrated our twenty-fifth wedding anniversary, I took her to the jeweler to buy her a special diamond. Of course, I didn't see what she saw, so several of the stones we considered looked fine to me. But she would say, "No, that one isn't right."

Finally, she found a diamond she liked and asked to see it. The jeweler did something very interesting when he brought out the diamond my wife wanted to see. Instead of just holding it in his hand, he laid it on a black velvet cloth. The cloth provided a backdrop for the diamond, which made it sparkle all the more brilliantly. You have to see a diamond against a dark backdrop to appreciate it fully.

Verses 1–3 of Ephesians 2 are the dark background against which Paul wants to show us the grace of God. And the background is very dark, because in our natural, unredeemed state, we were totally unacceptable to a holy God.

The words "trespasses and sins" give two different nuances to our sinful state. To trespass means to depart from the right way, and to sin means to miss the mark, as an archer misses the mark when he misses the bull's-eye. By nature we lived in an environment of sin and breathed the air of rebellion against God. If we really want to see where we were without Christ, we should visit the cemetery.

THE HEAVENLY CORONER'S REPORT

You see, what we have in Ephesians 2:1–3 is fundamentally a coroner's report. Among dead people there are different levels of decomposition. A person who has been dead a long time won't be looking so great, while someone else who has just died may still be looking pretty good in the casket. But both people are equally dead.

A lot of spiritually dead people don't feel dead. And as far as they and the people around them are concerned, they don't look dead. But those who are still in their sins are dead, according to God's Word.

We go to a lot of trouble to dress up death and take the edge off. But don't miss the point. We were dead in our sins, and Ephesians 2:2–3 says there were three nails in our coffin: the world, the "prince of the power of the air," or the devil, and our own sinful flesh. The bottom line is that we were cut off from the eternal life that Christ gives. And without Christ's sacrifice the only possibility is eternal death or separation from God in hell.

GOD'S GRACE MADE US ALIVE IN CHRIST

The "before" picture of our standing before God isn't pretty, but thank God there is also an "after" picture. Ephesians 2:4 begins with two of the most important, exciting, and life-changing words in the Bible. "But God" are words that will reverse any situation. "But God" will bring life where death existed, because of what God has done for us in grace.

We need to look at verses 4–5 to get the entire thought: "But God, being rich in mercy, because of His great love with which He loved us, even when we were dead in our transgressions, made us alive together with Christ (by grace you have been saved)."

That last phrase is the key. If you know Christ as your Savior, you are saved not because of your decision or anything else you did, but because God took the initiative to reach down and save you by grace.

If you took your children to a petting zoo and a little lamb came running toward you, you probably wouldn't be afraid at all. You might even reach out your hand for the lamb to lick.

But suppose you are at the zoo when the alarm goes out that a lion has escaped from its cage. If that lion came running toward you, you would be terrified and start to run because you know what lions can do. Now suppose the runaway lion corners you and comes at you—but instead of attacking you, the lion simply licks your hand gently the way the lamb did.

If that happened, whose gentleness would you appreciate more, the lamb's or the lion's? I would appreciate the lion's gentleness more because I know that he could just as easily have destroyed me without violating his nature as a lion at all.

Grace is God's kindness and gentleness to us when He could have backed us into a corner as guilty sinners and destroyed us without violating His holy character. But God wanted to make us His children, so instead of expressing His wrath against us, He poured it out on His own sinless Son on the cross. Jesus took our punishment so God could embrace us.

GOD HAS ADOPTED US

God's grace has a wonderful, lifelong goal that reaches even beyond His initial gift of salvation. "He predestined us to adoption as sons through Jesus Christ to Himself, according to the kind intention of His will" (Ephesians 1:5).

In other words, God determined that our destiny was to become His adopted children. For us as God's elect and His adopted children, this inheritance includes "every spiritual blessing in the heavenly places in Christ" (v. 3). As Christians, too many of us are still living in the spiritual ghetto even though our Daddy owns it all. We've not grown up to discover all of our rights and privileges in Christ.

The grace of God calls for a response on our part—not to try to pay for what we have but out of overflowing gratitude for what God has done for us. Let's talk about how we can grow in Christ, which the Bible calls the process of sanctification.

3

SANCTIFIED BY GRACE

Many of the Christians whom we could call "grace challenged" will work hard and go to great lengths trying to please God. They remind me of the young man in Brazil who crawled fourteen miles on his knees to his girlfriend's house to show her how much he loved her and how sorry he was for whatever he did to offend her. People lined the road to watch this man crawl to his girlfriend's, but when he arrived, she wasn't even there.

Growing in grace is a crucial issue, because the Bible commands us: "Grow in the grace and knowledge of our Lord and Savior Jesus Christ" (2 Peter 3:18). Besides, the only alternative to grace in the Christian life is self-effort, which can be as futile as that young Brazilian's long crawl to an empty house.

We love to sing songs about God's grace, but growing in grace each day is often another story. Why is this so hard to do? One reason is that grace is a foreign environment to us, much like a person moving to a foreign country and trying to get accustomed to the language and culture. The Bible says we have to grow in grace because it is not our normal orientation.

> THE ONLY ALTERNATIVE TO GRACE IN THE CHRISTIAN LIFE IS FUTILE SELF-EFFORT.

Because we were born in sin, no one had to show us how to act out our sinful nature. But we will spend the rest of our lives learning what it means to live by grace. The Bible never commands us, "Grow in the Law." You will never read in God's Word, "Become better at keeping the rules." It does command us to obey God, and growing in obedience is part of what it means to grow in grace. Grace and growth are two sides of the same coin. My goal in this section is to help you grow in grace.

A WONDERFUL GIFT

Learning about God's grace is like opening one of those huge, cellophane-wrapped gift baskets at Christmas. Every time you think you've found all the goodies in the basket, you reach in a little deeper and find something else good just waiting to be discovered and enjoyed.

That's what we are finding in Ephesians 2. It would have been enough if God had put a period after the tremendous declaration "By grace you have been saved" (v. 5). But grace doesn't stop there. After making us alive with Christ when we were dead, God took us to heaven with Jesus when He rose from the dead and ascended back to His place at God's right hand.

According to Ephesians 2:6, "[God] raised us up with Him, and seated us with Him in the heavenly places in Christ Jesus." There is a divine relocation program involved in grace, whereby God takes those people He has saved and seats them with Christ.

Now, in case you think this relocation is just a figure of speech or a nice thing that we will experience someday, notice the tense of the verbs. God "raised" us up and "seated" us with Christ, past tense. It's already been done. You may be living on earth, but your true existence is in heaven.

We know that Christ is seated at the right hand of God (see Hebrews 10:12), which is the position of power and divine favor. That means Jesus Christ can make any request of His Father and know that it will be granted. So if you need power, wisdom, strength in temptation, victory over sin, or any other spiritual blessing, you find them at God's right hand where Jesus is seated and you are seated with Him.

GOD'S ETERNAL KINDNESS

If you think the grace blessings God has for you today are wonderful, you haven't seen anything yet. Ephesians 2:7 is a whopper. Here Paul tells us why God loved us, saved us, raised us up with Christ, and seated us with Him in the heavenly places: "So that in the ages to come [God] might show the surpassing riches of His grace in kindness toward us in Christ Jesus."

Christian sister, imagine being married to a man whose every waking moment is spent doing new acts of kindness to prove his love for you. I know what you're thinking—*Where is he?*

This will never happen on earth, because nobody is capable of that kind of endless grace. But during the endless ages of eternity, God is going to show us the "surpassing riches of His grace." This is part of what will make heaven so glorious. Think of all that God has blessed you with on earth, and then try to imagine what His kindness will be like when all the limitations of earth are removed. God's grace will keep flowing in a never-ending stream, and no two gifts will be alike because He is infinite.

That's what God has waiting for us in heaven, and He has no problem telling us about it up front. And by the way, Christianity is the only religion that promises heaven up front. Other religions, and the cults, generally keep their followers in the dark about their future destiny so they can keep the troops in line and working hard to earn God's favor.

Don't get me wrong. This doesn't mean that as Christians we get off without working. But there's a world of difference between serving God out of gratitude for His grace and trying to earn His grace by our works. The moment you came to Christ, God brought you back from the dead and seated you with Jesus Christ in heaven. Your eternal future is secure, because heaven is included in the package called God's grace.

GOD'S SUPER-ABUNDANT GRACE

Perhaps you are thinking, *This sounds great, but how can I grab hold of the grace I need now to grow in Christ, endure trials, and live victoriously?*

I want to answer this with the most powerful verse about grace in the Bible. But first, let me clarify that the grace we are talking about here is not saving grace but grace to live the Christian life after you are saved. God's promise of abundant grace is found in a verse you ought to memorize if you haven't already: "God is able to make all grace abound to you, so that always having all sufficiency in everything, you may have an abundance for every good deed" (2 Corinthians 9:8).

THE GRACE IS RELATED TO YOUR NEED.

The specific context of this verse is our giving to

God's work, which is one important aspect of the Christian life. But take another look at the occurrences of the word *all* in this passage. They are a comprehensive statement of God's grace; the ability to give flows out of this abundance.

My point is that God's grace is as abundant here on earth as it is in heaven. The difference is that in heaven there are no challenges to grace, while down here there are plenty of things to distract us and keep us from taking hold of grace.

You see, God will always relate to you in grace, and He has all the grace you need. But the grace is related to your need. You don't get tomorrow's grace today. You don't get dying grace until you're dying. You don't get grace to face temptation until you're being tempted. God has grace available for every situation that is over and above the need. Make no mistake about it. God's throne is "the throne of grace" (Hebrews 4:16).

GRACE AND THORNS

What most people really want to know is, If God is so gracious, why doesn't He just take away the trial or the suffering? Why doesn't He keep the thorns from growing in our lives?

Paul gives us the answer in 2 Corinthians 12:7–10. He called one of his trials "a thorn in the flesh, a messenger of Satan to torment me—to keep me from exalting myself!" (v. 7). Paul's thorn could have been a physical problem, a person who caused him grief, or a problem with no solution. Whatever it was, God allowed it to persist to keep Paul humble and to teach him this valuable lesson: "My grace is sufficient for you, for power is perfected in weakness" (v. 9).

Paul had asked God three times to remove the thorn (see v. 8). God's answer was sufficient grace to endure the thorn and power to minister in spite of the weakness caused by the problem. Paul wanted God's grace and power more than he wanted relief, so he responded, "Therefore I am well content with weaknesses . . . for when I am weak, then I am strong" (v. 10).

So the question that needs to be asked is from God to us, not us to God. His question to us is, "Do you want to see My grace operating in super-abundant power in your life?"

If your answer is, "Yes, Lord, more than anything," then be ready to accept the thorns. When problems come, it means God is getting ready to show you more of His grace, because where He's taking you is greater than where you are now. All you need to know is that His grace is sufficient.

OUR RESPONSE TO GOD'S GRACE

We detoured from Ephesians 2 for a while to learn an important principle about the super-abundance of God's grace. Now we're ready to go back and look at Ephesians 2:8–10, which teaches us that anything we could possibly do for God is simply a response of gratitude to His grace, not a payment for it.

Paul writes, "For by grace you have been saved through faith; and that not of yourselves, it is the gift of God; not as a result of works, so that no one may boast" (Ephesians 2:8–9). Paul said God left the thorn in his flesh to keep him humble. God doesn't want us bragging about how we earned His favor.

But immediately after this great statement of salvation by faith through grace, we read these words: "For we are His workmanship, created in Christ Jesus for good works, which God prepared beforehand so that we would walk in them" (v. 10). Grace should not lead us to try to take advantage of God's goodness by sinning all we want, or by doing nothing while soaking up His favor. God has work for us to do, but He doesn't want us serving Him because we're trying to earn our own way. That is working against grace. God wants us to serve Him in response to His relationship of love and grace with us.

In discussing his own life, Paul said he "labored even more than all of them" (1 Corinthians 15:10), referring to the other apostles—although he added, "Yet not I, but the grace of God with me." Paul knew that he was created in Christ for good works, but his service for the Lord was not a burdensome duty. His goal in everything was to know Christ more intimately (see Philippians 3:10).

Grace is cultivated and grows by relationship, not

by rules or endless spiritual calisthenics. This is true because grace is not just a doctrine but a person (see John 1:16; Titus 2:11–12). The deeper our relationship with Christ, the greater the experience of grace and therefore the greater the spiritual growth.

If you are a parent, when your child falls down and skins her knee, do you go to the medicine chest, take out a list of things to do for skinned knees, read it off to your child, and say, "This is what I am obligated to do for you"?

Of course not. When your little girl hurts herself, you take her in your arms and wipe away her tears as you apply the healing solution, because your relationship is the driving force behind your actions. And your child responds in love to your gracious act. That's the response God wants from us.

4

Set Free by Grace

I hope you're getting the message that our Christian faith hinges on the truth that in Christ God has taken the initiative to save us—not only without our help but in spite of our sin and rebellion against Him. Paul said it well: "For while we were still helpless, at the right time Christ died for the ungodly" (Romans 5:6). People who are helpless and ungodly cannot set themselves free. God had to take the initiative to free us.

One of the Bible's greatest statements on grace is found in Titus 2:11–14. Paul told Titus to teach the churches under his charge this truth: "For the grace of God has appeared, bringing salvation to all men."

God's grace has existed from all eternity. Some liber-al theologians used to talk about the contrast between the God of wrath, vengeance, and judgment in the Old Testament and the God of love, grace, and forgiveness in the New Testament. No, God has always been a God of grace. The Old Testament is filled with stories of His gracious dealings with mankind. But before Christ appeared and sin was fully dealt with, we could say that God's grace was in the shadows. Like the sun on a cloudy day, God's grace was fully present before Christ, but it was not fully visible to us.

But when Christ came, it was like the clouds parting to reveal the sun in all of its glory. The grace of God appeared when Jesus came to earth. Jesus is the full-orbed expression of God's grace. John said of Jesus, "There was the true Light which, coming into the world, enlightens every man" (John 1:9). Jesus brought the saving purposes of God out of the shadows.

John then continued: "The Word became flesh, and dwelt among us, and we saw His glory, glory as of the only begotten from the Father, full of *grace* and truth" (v. 14, italics added). And finally: "For of His fullness we have all received, and *grace upon grace*. For the Law was given through Moses; *grace* and truth were realized through Jesus Christ" (vv. 16–17, italics added).

Grace is embodied in the person of Christ. And the grace He brought at the cross brings salvation "to all men." I need to explain this phrase, because it does not mean that everyone is going to heaven. The idea is that through His death on the cross Christ paid for all sin, including the universal condemnation all men inherited from Adam, which theologians call original sin. That means no person will go to hell for what Adam did in the Garden of Eden. Adam's corruption of the human race has been fully addressed in Christ. His death saved all men from original sin (Romans 5:18) and rendered all people "savable" regarding personal sin, so that anyone who goes to hell will go because of his or her own sin and refusal to accept Christ.

But for those of us who have accepted the grace of God in the person of Jesus Christ, God has opened a spiritual vault making available to us all of the resources needed to fulfill His purposes for our lives. All of it comes through the grace that appeared when Jesus came.

I don't know about you, but I would not want to have to relate to God on the basis of the Law. The Law came through Moses and instructed God's people about His demands. But the Law provided no power to keep it, and it prescribed severe penalties for anyone who broke it.

But the Bible says that when Christ came, He fulfilled the Law and released us from its condemnation. "Christ is the end of the law for righteousness to everyone who believes" (Romans 10:4). We should get on our knees and faces every day to thank God that His grace was fully and finally revealed in Jesus Christ.

THE TEACHING OF GRACE

The grace of God that has appeared in Christ has a lot to teach us. According to Titus 2:12, this grace "instruct[s] us to deny ungodliness and worldly desires and to live sensibly, righteously and godly in the present age." Grace not only redeems us; it reforms us. Living by grace opens up to us a whole new set of data that we were unaware of before. That's why we need to be instructed in the grace of God. It's an entirely new way of thinking and living.

We are quick to forget that God's grace is free. One way you can test any preacher (or any movement) is whether he wants you to pay for your manifestation of grace.

By that I mean if you have to send a gift to get a bottle of specially blessed water from the Jordan River so you can experience God's blessing, something is wrong. If you have to send for an anointed handkerchief in order to see God work in your life, that's not of God, because He relates to you in grace, and His grace is free. The Bible says, "He who did not spare His own Son, but delivered Him over for us all, how will He not also with Him freely give us all things?" (Romans 8:32). God freely gave us Christ, the most expensive grace gift ever given.

Grace also has a lot to teach us because some people will take God's grace to its illogical conclusion and say, "Since we are under grace and nothing can change that, let's sin to our hearts' content because we're already forgiven."

That argument is as old as Christianity. Paul addressed this issue in a classic passage that begins with these questions: "What shall we say then? Are we to continue in sin so that grace may increase?" (Romans 6:1). Then he gave the ringing answer: "May it never be! How shall we who died to sin still live in it?" (v. 2). Anyone who thinks grace is a license to sin doesn't understand the first thing about it.

RULES ALONE DON'T CHANGE THE HUMAN HEART.

We also have a strong answer to the "let us sin more" argument back in Titus 2:12. Grace teaches us to say no to ungodliness and yes to righteousness. Grace should motivate us to serve, not to sin. In fact, our service and dedication to God as people of grace ought to far outshine anything that was done under the Law. We serve in response to God's outpouring of favor upon us.

When grace gets hold of you, and when you really grasp the extent of what God did for you in Christ, no act of love or sacrifice God asks of you is too great.

Now if grace holds so much for us, it makes sense that this is the primary message Christians should be learning. But it's amazing how many believers are still in kindergarten when it comes to understanding grace. Unfortunately, too often this is the case because pastors do not clearly understand the truth of grace.

Here's one more reason that churches must be grace oriented and teach their members how to live the Christian life from this orientation. Grace is different from law not only because the basis of acceptance is different. Grace is also different because it has within it the power to enable believers to fulfill the instructions and demands of God's Word. In other words, grace enables what God expects.

That's important because God's expectations have never changed. God has always required that people say no to sin and yes to righteousness. But as we said above, the Law of Moses had no inherent power to enable our obedience. But in grace, God writes His law on our hearts by the Holy Spirit and gives us the Spirit to indwell and empower us. The church should be a powerhouse of obedient Christians who know how to tap into the Spirit's enabling grace to live for Christ. The world should be looking at us and saying, "If that's what living by grace can do, I want in on it!"

You see, the world is used to living by rules. But rules alone don't change the human heart. If your heart is diseased and beyond repair, no number of rules about not smoking and eating right will fix it. But if you receive a new heart through a transplant, nobody should have to lecture you about how to keep that heart working like new. You will respond in gratitude for your heart, which was a gift of grace that someone else provided.

Responding in obedience because of a relationship will always accomplish more than guilt-laced lectures rooted in rules alone. But too many Christians aren't experiencing this truth because the churches they attend don't teach it.

THE FOCUS OF GRACE

Once we experience the grace of God in Christ, everything changes, including our focus. If we are looking for grace, we won't find it by looking in the mirror or anywhere else except to Jesus. The writer of Hebrews called us to "[fix] our eyes on Jesus, the author and perfecter of faith" (Hebrews 12:2).

Paul had the same idea in Titus 2:13, which continues the great sentence he began in verse 11: "Looking for the blessed hope and the appearing of the glory of our great God and Savior, Christ Jesus." Jesus is the focus of grace; our eyes need to be firmly fixed on Him.

Now you may say, "But this verse tells us to be looking for Christ's return. What does this future hope have to do with our living by grace today?" Oh, that's the best part. It has everything to do with today because Christ wants His church to keep Him first in its focus. Jesus' parable of the talents teaches us to conduct our lives as if the Master of the house could return at any moment (see Matthew 25:14–30).

In other words, looking for Christ's return in glory does not mean that we sit around doing nothing because He might come back today, or live any old way we please because He might not come back for a long time. When we live with our eyes on Jesus, looking for the blessed hope of His return, we will start to become more like Him. John said this about people who hope to see Jesus someday: "Everyone who has this hope fixed on Him purifies himself, just as He is pure" (1 John 3:3).

In Titus 2:11, Paul said that God's grace appeared in Christ at His first coming as Savior. Now we look for the second appearance of Christ, who will bring grace to fulfillment when He gathers the church to Himself and we celebrate the marriage supper of the Lamb (see Revelation 19:1–9).

Besides the fact that Jesus is our glorious God and Savior, there is another reason for us to keep our focus on Him. Jesus is also perfect Man, who knows exactly where you are and where you are coming from because He has been there. There is no tight spot you will ever be in, and no temptation you will ever face, that Jesus did not face Himself (see Hebrews 4:14–16).

You say, "Yes, but that was Jesus. He's the perfect Son of God. I don't have His ability to be victorious over sin."

Yes, you do. Jesus is ministering in heaven today as your Great High Priest to enable you to be an overcomer. Listen to this incredible invitation: "Therefore let us draw near with confidence to the throne of grace, so that we may receive mercy and find grace to help in time of need" (Hebrews 4:16).

The reason more believers aren't living in the victory that is ours by grace is that we are looking through the wrong end of the binoculars, so to speak. If you have ever tried that, you know how impossible it is to see what you want to see. We look at ourselves and see how weak and small we are, instead of looking at Christ and how mighty and all-glorious He is.

Now, if you're wondering how you can get Christ in focus, the answer is found in your worship. I'm talking about a lifestyle in which you learn the secret that the psalmist knew: "I will bless the Lord at all times; His praise shall continually be in my mouth. My soul will make its boast in the Lord; the humble will hear it and rejoice" (Psalm 34:1–2). You look to Christ by faith in giving Him the glory He deserves.

WHEN GOD SAVES YOU BY HIS GRACE, THERE IS NOTHING HE CANNOT DO THROUGH YOU.

And when you do that, something important comes into focus. I love the next verse of Psalm 34: "O magnify the Lord with me, and let us exalt His name together" (v. 3). A magnifying glass makes an object look bigger to you. You can't make God any bigger than He is, since He already encompasses the universe. But you can make Him look bigger to you when you praise and worship Him.

THE PEOPLE OF GRACE

There is one more verse I want us to consider in Titus 2. Speaking of Jesus Christ, Paul continued, "Who gave Himself for us to redeem us from every lawless deed, and to purify for Himself a people for His own possession, zealous for good deeds" (v. 14). God's grace has taken a bunch of rebels against Him and turned us into His family.

The reason you and I are going to make it is that we are special to God. My office at church receives as many as one hundred telephone calls a day. But I have another line that only my family has access to, so that no matter what I am doing, family members can always get through if they need me, because they are special. God says we are family, with full access to His grace. And even when we fall, grace is there to catch us.

When God saves you by His grace, there is nothing He cannot do through you. Our motto ought to be "I can do all things through Him who strengthens me" (Philippians 4:13).

THE FREEDOM OF GRACE

Freedom is wonderful, especially when Jesus Christ sets you free. His own declaration is "If the Son makes you free, you will be free indeed" (John 8:36). The final blessing of grace is the freedom that it brings.

"It was for freedom that Christ set us free; therefore keep standing firm and do not be subject again to a yoke of slavery" (Galatians 5:1). If you have been set free by Jesus Christ, stand firm in your freedom, and don't let the devil put his yoke around your neck again.

Biblical freedom is the ability and the privilege God

gives you to fulfill your divinely ordained purpose. Jesus called it having life "abundantly" (John 10:10). He also said, "My yoke is easy and My burden is light" (Matthew 11:30). John wrote, "For this is the love of God, that we keep His commandments; and His commandments are not burdensome" (1 John 5:3). When grace is our motivation, there is joy in keeping God's commands.

Stand Firm in Your Freedom

So how do we experience the freedom Christ purchased for us on the cross? We need to get rid of that plantation mentality. Don't let anyone put a yoke of religious legalism on your neck.

This is serious stuff. You can't pick and choose which laws you want to obey. If you are going to try to please God by law keeping, you have to keep the whole Law, or the entire structure comes crashing down around you (see James 2:10). What's more, the Bible says, law and grace are mutually exclusive. Trying to live by the Law severs you from Christ, which is like cutting off the power cord to an appliance. This helps explain the powerlessness in so many churches in spite of the fact that they regularly teach the Bible.

When I go to the cafeteria, I always drink sweetened tea. There are two ways to make ice tea sweet. You can either take unsweetened tea and stir in your own sugar, or you can order tea that was sweetened by the restaurant staff when it was made. The problem with doing it yourself is that you never get the sugar all dissolved the right way, so there is always some residue at the bottom of the glass to make the last few gulps too sweet.

But when the restaurant staff sweetens the tea, the sugar is dissolved just right because they add it when the tea is brewing and the water is hot. That way the sugar becomes a component of the tea instead of a late add-on. When the Holy Ghost gets hold of you and the fire from heaven melts your heart, grace becomes a vital component of your walk with God and creates a relationship out of which good works come. You are not working to make it right but working because God made it right.

Paul told the Galatians not to abandon grace. There is no need to, because God's grace is inexhaustible. James says He gives "a greater grace" (James 4:6). Paul said that grace abounds to cover sin (see Romans 5:20). I want to finish this booklet by considering the sufficiency of grace.

5

The Sufficiency of Grace

Perhaps you know the story of the farmer who heard grand tales about the riches that were to be had for anyone who discovered oil. He heard about the oil that was supposed to be lying in abundance under the land in the far corners of the earth, just waiting to be discovered and make the finder fabulously rich.

So the farmer allowed his desire for wealth to get the better of him. He sold his farm and put everything he had into the effort to find oil, in hopes of enjoying a better life. But he spent years traveling the earth in a futile search for oil and returned home broke and discouraged.

It was only then that he learned the new owner of his farm had found a large reserve of oil on the property and had become fabulously wealthy. The former owner had owned great wealth all the time in the legal sense, but he never truly possessed or enjoyed his wealth because he forsook it to chase after a fruitless dream.

A lot of Christians today are like that impatient farmer. They're running all over the spiritual map looking for something to give them the edge in their Christian life—some spiritual "secret" that will unlock the fullness of God's riches. And all the time, they are sitting on God's riches in the form of His grace.

My friend, we don't begin the Christian life by grace and then move on to something better. Paul asked the Galatians: "Are you so foolish? Having begun by the Spirit, are you now being perfected by the flesh?" (Galatians 3:3). Your Christian life will take a giant leap forward when you fully understand grace and what it means in your life.

THE GIFT OF GRACE

The first thing I want us to see is the gift of grace. Understanding how grace works can be so powerful in helping to set you free for the reason suggested above. The best thing you can do with a gift is to receive it with gratitude. Let me give you several distinguishing marks of God's gift of grace.

Speaking of the remnant of Israel that believes in Christ, Paul said, "But if [this remnant] is by grace, it is no longer on the basis of works, otherwise grace is no longer grace" (Romans 11:6).

What is true of God's work with Israel is true of God's work with us. Human works, our own efforts to make ourselves acceptable to God, are so antithetical to grace that the two cancel each other out. Paul told the Galatians, "I do not nullify the grace of God, for if righteousness comes through the Law, then Christ died needlessly" (2:21).

Human works as epitomized in trying to keep the Law are not only counter to grace; they are counterproductive to grace. Remember, sin finds its power in the Law (see 1 Corinthians 15:56). Even though the Law isn't sinful, we are—so when our sinful flesh runs up against God's law, the flesh immediately wants to rebel and sin.

If you are a performance-based Christian—a legalist—you won't appreciate grace. In fact, your performance will cancel the very grace you pray for. A lot of Christians don't realize that after they get on their knees and ask God to help them, they get up off their knees and cancel that request by gritting their teeth and trying to perform to win God's approval.

Grace is not cheap, but it is free (see Revelation 22:17). The Bible says we are "justified as a gift by [God's] grace" (Romans 3:24). *Free* means no charge at all, no strings attached.

Suppose I invite you to dinner and we have a great evening, but when you get ready to go home I surprise you with a bill of fifty dollars for the meal. Our relationship would change drastically from one of grace to one of obligation. The meal would no longer be a gift of grace but merely a service for which I charge you a fee. What makes grace so marvelous is that it is absolutely free.

Grace is also an all-inclusive offer. The Bible says, "Blessed be the God and Father of our Lord Jesus Christ, who has blessed us with every spiritual blessing in the heavenly places in Christ" (Ephesians 1:3). Too many Christians accept Christ as Savior by grace but then seek to live the Christian life by the works of the Law. That's because they're confused about grace.

It's important to realize that the grace that saves us is not static. Grace assures us of heaven, but it also equips us for a life of spiritual growth and maturity here on earth. However, anytime you offer something extremely valuable free of charge, there is a risk attached. Grace is risky business.

As Paul explained God's grace to the church at Rome, he understood that some of his readers might wonder if grace was really all that marvelous, while others might try to abuse grace. So he wrote, "The Law came in so that the transgression would increase; but where sin increased, grace abounded all the more" (Romans 5:20). The Law of God shows us that we're far more sinful than we ever thought we were. But once we realize how bad off we are, and how far God's grace reaches beyond the extent of our sin, we won't have any doubts about the marvel of grace.

Paul also had a word for those who figured that the abounding nature of grace meant they could sin all they wanted to and then run to God for forgiveness. Their twisted argument was that sin was good because more sin released more grace.

Some people have taken that approach to the Christian life, in their actions if not in their words. The risk of grace is that some will try to take advantage of God's goodness.

> YOU KNOW YOU ARE LIVING IN GRACE WHEN THERE IS AN ABUNDANCE.

But God is willing to take that risk. His grace is so marvelous that He will give it to us and endure the pain of our misusing it. God is willing to take the risk of saving us freely and then having us forget how great the gift of salvation is (see 2 Peter 1:9).

Do you know how I know that grace could come from God alone? Because if most of us gave something very precious to people and they began abusing it or forgetting to say thanks, we would stop giving and say, "That's it. No more gift." Thank God that He doesn't do that with us.

Grace is not only a gift; it is a *great* gift. Paul almost ran out of superlatives describing grace in 2 Corinthians 9:8: "God is able to make all grace abound to you, so that always having all sufficiency in everything, you may have an abundance for every good deed."

You know you are living in grace when there is an abundance. You don't just have joy, but "joy inexpressible and full of glory" (1 Peter 1:8). Not just peace, but "peace . . . which surpasses all comprehension" (Philippians 4:7).

GETTING THE GIFT OF GRACE

Since grace is such a great gift, we need to know how to get our hands on it. Many Christians have been saved by grace but do not know how to make the grace that saved them a reality in their daily walk with Christ.

Jesus gave us the key to putting grace to work when He said, "Abide in Me, and I in you. As the branch cannot bear fruit of itself unless it abides in the vine, so neither can you unless you abide in Me. . . . For apart from Me you can do nothing" (John 15:4–5).

"Abiding" is a word we don't hear very often these days, but people use another word that has the same basic meaning: bonding. People talk about bonding with another person, forming a connection that brings the two people together in a vital, even life-changing, relationship.

That's the kind of relationship Jesus wants to have with us, so we can produce the fruit His grace wants to produce in us.

We get the gift of grace for each day the same way we got the gift of grace for our salvation: by receiving it freely from Christ. That's why the Bible tells us, "Therefore as you have received Christ Jesus the Lord, so walk in Him" (Colossians 2:6). The Christian life is a grace adventure from first to last.

When you receive the gift of grace for daily Christian living, you no longer just pray, "Lord, I don't want to tell a lie today," but, "Lord, I give You the freedom to express Your truth through me."

Grace gets you beyond just praying, "Lord, I'm going to try not to yield to lust today." Instead, you're able to pray, "Lord, by Your grace I allow You to express Your purity of mind through me today."

When you start living like this, really living by grace, you wind up doing things you never thought you could do. You wind up loving folk you couldn't stand before. You wind up being able to control things in your life you couldn't control before. The key to grace living is not more self-effort and trying harder but getting closer to Christ. That's where the power is, as Paul knew so well. His passion in life was "That I may know [Christ] and the power of His resurrection" (Philippians 3:10).

POWER THAT NEVER RUNS LOW

I'm learning how to use a computer. I've already learned one basic fact, which is that there are two ways to power a computer. You can run it on a battery, which runs down and needs recharging, or you can plug your computer into an ever-flowing power source.

The problem with the battery is that if you forget to recharge it, or can't get to a power source to recharge it, your computer will eventually stop working.

Too many Christians are living by battery power

instead of God's ever-flowing grace. They come to church on Sunday to get spiritually recharged, but they begin to run out of power, so they have to come on Wednesday night for a midweek recharge. If they miss a week, watch out, because their spiritual battery is dangerously low.

But when you plug that computer into a permanent power source, an abiding takes place. The power never runs low because there is a connectedness between the computer and its power source that becomes a way of life.

Just in case you're beginning to think that the life of grace sounds pretty passive, with nothing for us to do, we need to look at two crucial verses that clarify the relationship between the good works God wants us to do and the grace we need to do them.

"So then, my beloved, just as you have always obeyed, not as in my presence only, but now much more in my absence, work out your salvation with fear and trembling; for it is God who is at work in you, both to will and to work for His good pleasure" (Philippians 2:12–13).

This is a passage you need to read all the way through, because if you quit at verse 12 you may get the idea that the Christian life depends on what you do. But the only reason we can work out our salvation is that God is working within us. In terms of our lives, verse 13 actually comes before verse 12, since the key to this is what God is doing in grace. Everything we do is simply an expression of His work.

Works and grace are mutually exclusive when it comes to salvation, but they have an important relationship in a Christian's life. When grace is at work, the works we do for the Lord are inspired and enabled by grace. It's not that we're working to gain God's favor, but we're working out what He has already worked in.

To put it another way, both the Old and the New Testament command us not to lie (Exodus 20:16; Colossians 3:9). The difference is that the Law states it as a command, period. The command is just as strong under grace, because God's standards do not change.

But because we are operating under grace, God's commands become an opportunity to display the character of Christ through us as we draw on the power of God working within us. This is how we activate the gift of grace for daily living.

THE GIVER OF GRACE

The secret to this "super grace" is allowing Christ to live out His perfect, sinless life through us in the power of His resurrection. The fact is that we are saved by Christ's sinless life as well as by His atoning death. The goal of the Christian life is "that the life of Jesus . . . may be manifested in our mortal flesh" (2 Corinthians 4:11).

The combination of Christ's righteousness and resurrection power in you is more than enough to put grace to work in your life. With all that power and perfection at work within you, all you have to do is cooperate with the workings of God in grace. As you yield yourself to Christ, He will fill you with the incredible, life-giving gift of grace.